WHAT IS ICING?

Common Hockey Questions Answered

EJ GREENLYN

Contents

Introduction

Let's. Do. That. Hockey! Wait…that's not it. As Lazlo Holmes has shown us—while hockey's popularity has steadily increased in the United States, it remains a bit of a niche sport. It has a devout fan base, but it isn't nearly as mainstream in the U.S. as other sports like baseball or football. The devotees watch their team and others on TV or via streaming services, while those who aren't intimately familiar with the game can't bring themselves to watch a full game on TV. Yet, nearly everyone reports having a great time attending a live hockey game. Why is that?

Well, hockey is a fast-paced, high intensity game. When you experience the intensity and find yourself surrounded by (mostly) knowledgeable fans, you can feel the energy of the game. When you watch a game in-person, you can overlook some of the whistles or movement you don't understand—after all, it's still moving quickly, and someone is yelling or cheering about it. But, if you're at home watching the game and you aren't familiar with the rules, it can seem quite slow between goals. When you begin to understand the rules and gameplay, you begin to see how fast the game really is and, after some time, you'll begin to enjoy watching at home.

Of course, to further complicate matters, the rules and even the rink size vary depending on the level of hockey—youth, college, Olympics, foreign leagues, or National Hockey League ("NHL"). Here we focus on NHL. While some of us die-hard hockey fans appreciate the niche nature of hockey, we're always happy to talk to someone about hockey and encourage them to learn more. This book aims to answer some of the most common questions that new fans have and offers a "refresher" on a few things for the hockey-savvy reader.

What is hockey?

A hockey game is played on an ice rink surrounded by low walls with glass atop (called "the boards"). There are three periods of twenty minutes each. The time is not running—the clock stops if the whistle blows. Between each period, the players and equipment leave the ice for an intermission period of twenty minutes, and the Zamboni cleans the ice. Also, the teams alternate ends after every period. Although the teams do not alternate benches, the goalies switch ends/nets each period. If a goalie was on the left end of the ice in the first period, he will be on the right end of the ice in the second period and return to the left end of the ice in the third period. This alternating pattern continues into overtime.

Each team has a total of twenty players for each game, consisting of eighteen skaters and two goalies. This is called the team's line-up. In regular play, each team has five skaters, plus a goalie on the ice. For the skaters, there are two defensemen and three forwards—left wing, right wing, and center. A team will designate one player as captain and one or two players as alternate captains. If there is no captain, the team may designate three players as alternate captains. This may change from year-to-year, or it may be the same individuals. Teams decide for themselves how captains and alternates will be determined. The three forwards that play together are called a "line" and the two defensemen who play together are called "partners"; however, you may also sometimes hear the entire grouping of five players on the ice together (three forwards and two defensemen) be called a "line."

With that very high-level summary, let's dive in to some more specific questions. To guide you, we will define various terms throughout the text, but you should also consult the glossary at the end of this book; it will give you definitions of some key hockey lingo as well as an explanation of some words that we use in this book.

How is the NHL organized and who are the teams?

The league began in 1942 with six teams—commonly referred to now as the "Original Six." These teams were the Boston Bruins, the Chicago Blackhawks, the Detroit Red Wings, the Montréal Canadiens, the New York Rangers, and the Toronto Maple Leafs. Since then, the league has seen significant expansion and has revised its structure of conferences and divisions multiple times, most recently with an overhaul in the 2013-14 season.

Currently, there are two conferences—the Eastern Conference and the Western Conference. Each has two divisions. The Eastern Conference is made up of the Atlantic and Metropolitan Divisions. These divisions are made up of eight teams each. The Western Conference is made up of the Pacific and Central Divisions. The Pacific Division has eight teams and the Central Division has seven teams. This structure has been established since the 2013-14 season, except that the Pacific Division only had seven teams until

2016-17 when a new expansion team in Las Vegas joined the league. Another new expansion team—the Seattle Kraken—will be incorporated into the league in the 2021-22 season. When this happens, Seattle will join the Pacific Division, and Arizona will move to the Central Division, which will give all divisions an equal number of eight teams. On the next page is the breakdown:

Eastern Conference-
Atlantic Division
Boston Bruins
Buffalo Sabres
Detroit Red Wings
Florida Panthers
Montréal Canadiens
Ottawa Senators
Tampa Bay Lightning
Toronto Maple Leafs

Western Conference-
Central Division
Arizona Coyotes
**Starting 2021-22
Chicago Blackhawks
Colorado Avalanche
Dallas Stars
Minnesota Wild
Nashville Predators
St. Louis Blues
Winnipeg Jets

<u>Eastern Conference-</u>
<u>Metropolitan Division</u>
Carolina Hurricanes
Columbus Blue Jackets
New Jersey Devils
New York Islanders
New York Rangers
Philadelphia Flyers
Pittsburgh Penguins
Washington Capitals

<u>Western Conference-</u>
<u>Pacific Division</u>
Anaheim Ducks
Arizona Coyotes
**Leaving in 2021-22
Calgary Flames
Edmonton Oilers
Los Angeles Kings
San Jose Sharks
Seattle Kraken
**Starting 2021-22
Vancouver Canucks
Vegas Golden Knights

What is an affiliate or farm team?

The NHL also has relationships with minor hockey leagues. This includes the American Hockey League ("AHL") and the East Coast Hockey League ("ECHL"). Each NHL team is affiliated with an AHL team, and most NHL teams are affiliated with an ECHL team. AHL and ECHL teams are "farm teams." This means that NHL teams have agreements with their minor league affiliates to request players to play in the NHL when needed, such as when a player on an NHL team is injured or otherwise unable to play.

For example, if an NHL team encounters an injury, the team may "call up" a player from the AHL to play on the NHL team in lieu of the injured player. The reverse also is true—the NHL can send minor league players back to their minor league teams if they are not performing to expectations or if the player for whom they were filling in returns. Depending how an NHL player's contract is written, an NHL team also may be able to send one of its own players to its affiliated AHL team for "conditioning." This can happen for several reasons, such as for a new player/rookie who needs more experience, a player who has had an extended absence due to injury, or a player who is not performing as expected.

AHL and ECHL teams each play full seasons—the AHL's season is seventy-six games and the ECHL's season is seventy-two games. The seasons are played concurrent with an NHL season, so if a player from an AHL or ECHL team is called up to the affiliate NHL team, the affected AHL or ECHL team is required to adjust their roster for their own games. In cases of an injury or illness, the NHL may request a player on a short timeframe. For this reason, many of the AHL teams are located in relatively close proximity to their affiliate NHL team.

Teams in the AHL compete for the Calder Cup, while teams in the ECHL compete for the Kelly Cup. Both leagues have several categories of awards and trophies for teams and for individuals. The categories tend to follow the categories of awards available in the NHL, with awards for most valuable player, best goaltender, community service, and so on.

When an NHL team is not affiliated with an AHL team, players are assigned to AHL teams affiliated with other NHL teams. Because the Seattle Kraken has not yet started playing (or drafted a team), they do not yet have any AHL or ECHL affiliations.

However, it has been reported that Seattle will be affiliated with a new expansion AHL team to be based in Palm Springs. It is expected that the AHL team also will begin in the 2021-22 season. The AHL and ECHL affiliations are shown in the chart below.

Minor League Affiliations		
NHL Team	AHL Team	ECHL Team
Anaheim Ducks	San Diego Gulls	Tulsa Oilers
Arizona Coyotes	Tucson Roadrunners	Rapid City Rush
Boston Bruins	Providence Bruins	Atlanta Gladiators
Buffalo Sabres	Rochester Americans	Cincinnati Cyclones
Calgary Flames	Stockton Heat	Kansas City Mavericks
Carolina Hurricanes	Charlotte Checkers	Greenville Swamp Rabbits
Chicago Blackhawks	Rockford Icehogs	Indy Fuel
Colorado Avalanche	Colorado Eagles	Utah Grizzlies
Columbus Blue Jackets	Cleveland Monsters	N/A
Dallas Stars	Texas Stars	Idaho Steelheads
Detroit Red Wings	Grand Rapids Griffins	Toledo Walleye
Edmonton Oilers	Bakersfield Condors	Wichita Thunder

Minor League Affiliations		
NHL Team	**AHL Team**	**ECHL Team**
Florida Panthers	Springfield Thunderbirds	N/A
Los Angeles Kings	Ontario Reign	N/A
Minnesota Wild	Iowa Wild	Allen Americans
Montréal Canadiens	Laval Rocket	N/A
Nashville Predators	Milwaukee Admirals	Florida Everblades
New Jersey Devils	Binghamton Devils	Adirondack Thunder
New York Islanders	Bridgeport Sound Tigers	Worcester Railers
New York Rangers	Hartford Wolf Pack	Maine Mariners
Ottawa Senators	Belleville Senators	Brampton Beast
Philadelphia Flyers	Lehigh Valley Phantoms	Reading Royals
Pittsburgh Penguins	Wiles-Barre/ Scranton Penguins	Wheeling Nailers
San Jose Sharks	San Jose Barracuda	N/A
Seattle Kraken	TBD—Palm Springs Expansion	N/A
St. Louis Blues	San Antonio Rampage	N/A

Minor League Affiliations		
NHL Team	**AHL Team**	**ECHL Team**
Tampa Bay Lightning	Syracuse Crunch	Orlando Solar Bears
Toronto Maple Leafs	Toronto Marlies	Newfoundland Growlers
Vancouver Canucks	Utica Comets	Kalamazoo Wings
Vegas Golden Knights	Henderson Silver Knights	Fort Wayne Komets
Washington Capitals	Hershey Bears	South Carolina Stingrays
Winnipeg Jets	Manitoba Moose	Jacksonville Icemen

How is an NHL season structured?

The regular season consists of eighty-two games. This includes forty-one homes games and forty-one away or road games. Away games tend to be more challenging because a team has certain benefits being on "home ice", like a cheering crowd, no need for travel, and faceoff advantage. The league endeavors to even things up by having each team play every other team at least once, every other team in its conference two to three times, and every team in its division four to five times. But, it can be difficult to schedule games evenly, so sometimes teams end up with long stretches of time at home, while others may end up with long stretches of time away. Multiple consecutive away games played on a team's "road trip" can pose a disadvantage to that team, particularly if they are playing home teams that are well-rested.

How is a game organized?

As noted above, each game consists of three periods of twenty minutes each. There is an intermission between each period of eighteen minutes. If a game goes into overtime and/or a shootout in regular season (as described below), there is no intermission period between the third period and overtime. On the other hand, if a game goes into overtime during playoffs, there is a twenty-minute intermission between the third period and the first overtime period, and if there is more than one overtime period, there will be an intermission period between any such overtime periods. Games do not end in a tie in the regular reason or the playoffs. Overtime periods and the shootout are described below.

Who plays in a game?

The overall team line-up is generally consistent from game-to-game, but the lines are shuffled around based on how players are performing and who the team is playing. Also, players may be swapped out occasionally based on performance or injuries. Each line typically plays in "shifts" that average 30 seconds to 1 minute, but they can play 30-40 shifts per game (some players play even more). What a shift lacks in duration it makes up for in speed and intensity. A team may change one player or an entire line at a whistle, but they often change one-by-one while the game is ongoing. This is called changing "on the fly."

As noted above, each team has five skaters and one goalie on the ice (except in penalty situations). This includes two defensemen and three forwards—center, right wing, and left wing. There are four lines of defensemen and of forwards. Typically, the first line is expected to be the top scoring line and tends to generate the most scoring opportunities. The fourth line is less often known as a goal-scoring line and often may be grittier than the other lines. But, these stereotypes are not always correct, and, in fact, each line's role can vary from game-to-game. Lines are not necessarily made up of the most talented players in order of their lines, but rather, which players play the best together. This tends to lead to the most goals and may help to reflect talent. Yet, coaches often "shake up the lines" or move players amongst lines, especially if a team or line is not performing up to expectations. Switching the lines can help to find which players have better chemistry with one another or help to motivate players who are moved "up" or "down" a line.

Each player is expected to play their position, though sometimes they are caught off-guard while not in position. For example, defensemen typically play closest to their goalie when on the ice. They will be near the goalie and net when protecting in the defensive zone, though that may include pulling away to chase an opposing player away. When in the offensive zone, defensemen typically are found just inside the blue line (hence why they are sometimes called "blueliners"). Though, again, in some cases, defensemen can be found away from the blue line when attempting to make a play. When a defenseman moves in toward the net in place of a forward for an offensive move, it is said that the defenseman is "deep in the zone" or "pinching in," meaning they are closer to the opposing goalie than they ordinarily would be.

In broad terms, a center's main goals are to win/control faceoffs, support offensive play through the middle of the ice, and interchange with other players as appropriate. The center is like a team's quarterback, if you will; he tends to direct the play generally. The wings may be called upon to take the center's place if necessary, such as if the center is kicked out of a faceoff. (Faceoffs are described in more detail below.) Otherwise, wings generally support offensive play from either side of the rink. All forwards support defensively as needed. For example, if a defenseman loses their stick while the play is in the defensive zone, a forward will give the defenseman their stick and play without one until the forward can get back to the bench for a replacement.

Goalies are tasked with playing in position, like skaters. This means that the goalie is expected to stand or kneel in a certain way and in a certain direction based on where the puck is and where the gameplay is occurring. For example, if a player is skating up the side of the rink, the goalie will move to that side of the net and face the player at an angle. This positioning is intended to give the goalie the best opportunity to stop the puck if the player shoots. If the goalie were on the *other* side of the net in this example, he would be out of position.

Aside from playing in position, goalies also have goaltending styles determining how they play. There are three main styles: butterfly, stand-up, and hybrid. Originally, goalies followed the stand-up style. This means that they played largely standing on their feet. It is largely obsolete. In contrast, butterfly means that a player often plays on his knees to protect the lower part of the net. This is a pretty common approach by goalies today. In between stand-up and butterfly is the hybrid approach. There are varying degrees, but a hybrid goalie typically is one who mixes his play with butterfly and stand-up play. One form of hybrid goalie is called a "profly" or "blocking" goalie; this refers to a goalie who (1) seeks to take up as much of the net as he can to make saves (2) tends to use the butterfly style most of the time, and (3) can move cleanly while in butterfly stances.

When skaters play in position, they are following their roles and playing where they should be based on the specific play they are making (where "play" means a determined arrangement like a Hail Mary in football). However, skaters may be forced out of position for many reasons, such as to defend an unexpected attack or to take advantage of a potential scoring opportunity like a breakaway. A breakaway occurs when a skater is skating ahead of the other players, including the other team's defense, toward the offensive zone and the opposing team's net. Sometimes a person on the breakaway will be said to be "in alone." This means that there are no other skaters in the zone with that player.

What is all that gear?

Although some terms are addressed in the glossary, it's helpful to understand the equipment, gear, and apparel involved in hockey as you read through the other sections. Following is a list of some key items:

Helmets

All players must wear one. Some helmets have a plexiglass visor in the front covering the forehead, but most skaters do not wear a full mask or "cage". Plexiglass visors are required for rookies who have played fewer than twenty-five games, and other players may opt to have them. Typically, you will only see this type of mask when a skater has had a significant facial injury. If a skater's helmet falls off, gameplay will continue. The skater is expected to leave the ice or retrieve and wear his helmet. A penalty may be assessed if he does not.

As you might expect, goalies wear helmets with full facemasks. If a goalie's helmet comes off, gameplay immediately stops. Goalie helmets are known for having intricate designs and artwork, sometimes with fan input and sometimes of their own design.

Jerseys

All players wear jerseys or "sweaters." The team logo is on the front, while the person's number and last name are on the back. The player's number also appears on the arms.

Skater Apparel

Each skater has skates, a helmet, jersey, shoulder pads, gloves, breezers, shin guards, and a stick.

Breezers

Special padded shorts that skaters wear. They allow skaters to have freedom of movement, while also providing some extra protection that the player otherwise would not have.

Sticks

They must be made of wood or another approved material. Most sticks are carbon fiber. Skaters often have different length sticks based on their height. Sticks also may be designed for a left- or right-handed shooter, such as by changing the curve of the blade. Players may not hold more than one stick, even if seeking to simply return a dropped stick to another player. They also must immediately drop a broken stick once they know it is broken. A goalie's stick has a much wider blade and a shorter shaft. If a goalie loses his stick during gameplay or if his stick breaks, a teammate can give the goalie his stick to use.

Goalie Gear

Helmet, jersey, stick, skates, chest and arm pads, breezers, knee pads, glove, blocker, and goalie pads (leg guards).

Goalie Glove

Typically worn by the goalie in his secondary hand. It's a catching glove, used to catch and hold (or "freeze") the puck.

Blocker

Pad worn on the goalie's dominant arm, the one in which the goalie holds his stick.

Goalie Pads

These are leg pads a goalie wears on each leg. They are used to protect the goalie's legs and to stop the puck. The league has changed the size of the pads on a few occasions to increase scoring.

Net

Each net is held in place by removable posts in holes in the ice. The whistle will be blown if a net is moved/knocked off of its proper place. If the goalie intentionally does it, he will get a penalty. The top of the net is called the crossbar. The sides of the net are called the posts. When the puck hits the crossbar or post, you often hear a distinctive ringing sound, to the relief of the goalie and to the dismay of the skater who shot the puck. If the puck bounces off the crossbar or post and into the net, it is a goal. However, the puck must go in the front side of the net. If it somehow goes in from underneath the back or side of the net, there will be no goal.

What is the deal with all those lines and dots on the ice?

To help understand hockey, it is crucial to understand the rink, the lines, and what areas make up what "zones." A standard regulation NHL rink is 200 feet long and 85 feet wide. As noted above, NHL games are played on ice rinks surrounded by the boards. Netting is at the top of the glass on each end of the arena as a security precaution. As you will hear and/or see at any hockey game, "Watch for flying pucks!" This is true, especially if you sit on the sides or corners of the arena—areas that do not have netting above the glass. You should take it seriously—pucks can travel over 100 mph.

Let's examine the layout of the rink on the next page and then walk through each of its components. A few labels have been added to help guide you.

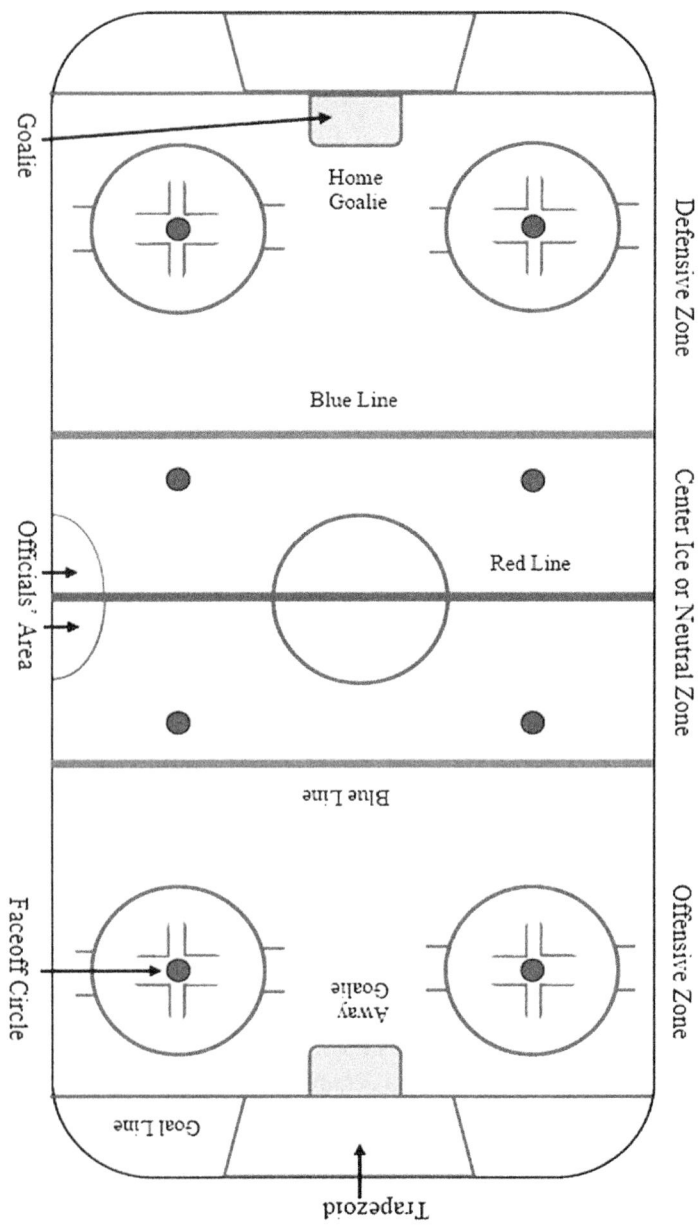

Goalie

Home
Goalie

Defensive Zone

Blue Line

Center Ice or Neutral Zone

Officials' Area

Red Line

Blue Line

Faceoff Circle

Offensive Zone

Away
Goalie

Goal Line

Trapezoid

It may seem like there is a lot going on in this picture, but we can break it down into manageable segments. Let's start with lines.

The red line in the center of the rink is called the "red line." The center circle on the red line is the location of the first faceoff of each period and after a goal is scored. The circle typically is branded for the home team. Where a player who plays the puck is in comparison to the red line determines whether icing has occurred. We'll talk more about icing later.

The two red lines at the ends of the rink are called the "goal lines." The goal lines serve two main purposes. First, as the name suggests, a goal line helps to determine whether a valid goal is scored. For a goal to be scored, the puck must enter the net <u>and</u> completely cross the goal line. Second, as with the red line, the goal lines help to determine whether a play is icing.

Each of the two blue lines on either side of the center red line is aptly called the "blue line." Each blue line serves to mark the zones. There are three main zones—neutral zone (also called center ice), attack/offensive zone, and defensive/defending zone. The area of the ice between the two blue lines is called the neutral zone or center ice. The area between the blue line and the goal is either a team's offensive zone or defensive zone depending where their goalie is. If the team's goalie is at the net on the left end of the rink as is the case in the above example, that end of the rink from the blue line to behind the net is the team's defensive zone (for the time when their goalie is on that side). Then, as illustrated in this example, the team's offensive zone would be the right end of the rink, where they would shoot on the opposing team's goalie (again, for the time when the opposing goalie is on that side). The end of the ice that serves as a team's offensive zone twice during a regular game is called the "double attack zone." [Pro tip: This is the best end of the arena to sit and watch a live game. You can see more closely your team's offensive efforts for two periods (i.e. two-thirds of the game).]

The set of angled lines behind the goalie's net constitutes the trapezoid. The trapezoid is the area in which the goalie can play the puck when behind the goal line. If the goalie plays the puck while it is outside the trapezoid in either corner behind the goal line, a penalty will be assessed (called "delay of game"). The semi-circle in front of the net is the goalie's "crease." This is the area where the goalie can move freely, so if a player on the other team checks/hits the goalie, a penalty called goaltender interference is assessed. The goalie is protecting his net, which is four feet tall and six feet wide. As noted above, the vertical sides of a net are called the "posts" and the horizontal top of the net is called the "crossbar"

In addition to the lines, you'll notice several circles with dots in the middle. Those are the faceoff circles and faceoff dots, respectively. A faceoff is the process by which play is re-initiated after play is stopped by a whistle. Those are the designated places in the rink where a faceoff may occur. Any faceoffs, other than the first one in the period or after a goal, are determined based on where the play was stopped and each team's actions. See below for more detail on faceoffs.

On either side of the ice are the team benches and the penalty boxes. There are two penalty boxes—one on each side of the red line inside the blue lines. In the example illustration, the penalty boxes would be on the side of the rink at the bottom of the image on either side of the officials' area at center ice. The benches would be directly across from the penalty boxes on the side of the arena at the top of the image.

Skaters move freely around the different zones of the ice. However, when a skater is in a certain area of the ice, this can affect the officiating. For example, as described below, where players are on the ice determines whether there is an icing or offsides call. Skaters will take different strategic formations throughout the game, but they are expected to play "in position." This means that a skater will play in the area of the ice and/or in the fashion expected of someone with that playing position (i.e. right wing or defenseman). A skater's position may not be immediately evident throughout gameplay, but you can determine the skater's position during a faceoff other than in the midst of a penalty, when both teams play with particular lines called "special teams." (More on special teams later.) The skater who takes the faceoff generally is the center. The skater to his left is the left wing and the skater to his right is the right wing. The two players farther behind are the defensemen.

What is a faceoff?

A faceoff occurs when a referee (ref) or linesman drops the puck between the sticks of two players—one from each team. The faceoff occurs in the faceoff circle and the puck is dropped on the faceoff dot. The players in the faceoff are usually centermen, though any player on the ice, except a goalie, can participate in a faceoff. As noted above, at the beginning of a period or after a goal is scored, the faceoff is always at the faceoff circle at center ice. However, any other faceoffs are determined based on the most recent play just before the whistle. For example, if the play was in the offensive zone for a team, but such team engaged in an illegal move that resulted in the whistle (such as a hand pass), the play may be moved outside the offensive zone to a different faceoff circle.

As for the process, once the official indicates that he is ready to drop the puck, both players have five seconds to get in position on either side of the faceoff circle. When the faceoff occurs at any circle other than the one at center ice, the defending player will place his stick on the ice first. If the faceoff is at center ice, the player from the away team will place his stick on the ice first. The puck will not be dropped until the home team player puts his stick on the ice. It is considered an advantage when the other player is required put his stick on the ice first (the "faceoff advantage"). This is because the advantaged player knows the precise moment when the puck will be dropped—when he puts his own stick down. Having the faceoff advantage is considered one of the "home advantages" for the home team.

If any of the below occur, the offending player will be "kicked out" of the faceoff, meaning that he will not be able to take the faceoff and he will need to trade places with one of the other skaters on the ice.

- The player is not in position at the dot within five seconds.
- The player does not have their stick on the ice when required.
- One of the player's teammates encroaches into the space near the dot.
- The player or one of his teammates touches an opposing player.
- Any player is in an offsides position.

Additionally, if a player touches the puck with his hand during or in connection with the faceoff, he will get a minor penalty. This includes swatting the puck with the hand or covering the puck with a hand (the latter of which is never allowed).

Why was the whistle blown?

There are many reasons why the whistle may be blown and play may be stopped. Some common examples are below.

- Puck is played with a high-stick or hand pass.
- Puck goes out of play.
- Serious injury.
- Net knocked off its place.
- Goalie loses his helmet.
- Goalie freezes/stops the puck.
- Goal.
- Icing.
- Offsides.
- Penalty.

The puck may not be played with a high-stick or off a hand pass. Although a skater may bat the puck out of the air with a stick or knock it to the ice with his hand, his teammate may not play the puck off of the high-stick or hand pass. If a teammate tries to play the puck off of a high-stick or hand pass, the whistle will be blown. However, if the skater or a member of the opposing team touches the puck with the stick after the high-stick or hand pass, one of the skater's teammates may then play the puck without a whistle.

If the puck goes out of bounds (meaning that it goes into one of the benches or over the glass) or the net was knocked off its place, the whistle will be blown. Either could also result in a penalty depending on the circumstances. If the puck was shot over the glass by a defending player while in his defensive zone, a penalty will be issued. Similarly, if a defending player knocks his net off the post while in his defensive zone, a penalty will be issued.

If a player is very seriously injured and/or if a player is injured and the play cannot be advanced in the area where the player is on the ice, the play will be stopped. Also, if the goalie loses his helmet, the whistle will be blown.

If a goalie freezes the puck or if a goal is scored, the whistle is blown. Additionally, if there is icing, offsides, or a penalty, the whistle will be blown. These will be discussed in more detail separately below.

Like some other sports, a coach will <u>not</u> get a whistle or stoppage in play by calling a timeout. Rather, a timeout may only be called if play has already stopped. Each coach is allotted one thirty-second timeout per game. Timeouts are typically taken in situations where (a) the opposing team has been playing dominantly and/or scored one or more goals, (b) the players on the ice are tired and the coach wants to give them a brief rest so they can continue playing (perhaps during a penalty kill or powerplay), (c) when the team does not seem to be playing well or is not following direction, or (d) near the end of the game to discuss plays when the team is seeking to tie the game to force overtime. Although in some cases, the coach wants to provide guidance to the players about a potential play, timeouts are often taken to give players a moment to rest or to allow players to regroup.

What is icing?

Icing and offsides are known to plague the casual observer. They are not penalties, but they do stop the play and have drawbacks for the team that makes the offending play.

As an initial matter, note that "icing" can be used as both a noun and a verb. It is a noun when someone refers to the infraction that occurred (i.e. that call was icing). It is a verb when someone refers to a player's action when committing the infraction (i.e. he iced the puck on the play). Icing occurs when one team shoots the puck across the red line from its defensive end to the other end of the ice, across the opposing team's goal line. A play will not be deemed icing if a player touches the puck after the initial shot/pass. Intent does not matter. If there is a missed pass or the player simply shoots the puck harder than intended, it is still icing.

If one of the offending team's players touches the puck at center ice or gets to the puck before a player on the opposing team, icing will be "waived off", meaning that the whistle will not be blown on the play and the offending team will face any consequences. Icing also will be waived off if the non-offending team's defensemen were "pinching in" in the offensive zone. Icing is waived off in this circumstance because, as the argument goes, if the defenseman had been in normal position near the blue line, he may have intercepted the puck and there may not have been icing at all.

Icing also will not be called on a team that is short-handed during a penalty (see below for more information on penalties).

For many years, the icing rule stated that the first player to actually touch the puck would determine whether icing was called. Although that created quite a bit of excitement as you watched players race for the puck, having players skate at top speed from one end of the arena to the other in a race to touch the puck was quite dangerous. It resulted in innumerable collisions, with players hitting one another after skating at full speed across the arena. As one may expect, this led to several injuries, and in some cases, significant injuries. Though a few such hits may have been intentional, most were unintentional. It is hard to stop at the drop of a hat when you've been skating full speed.

In recent years, for player safety, the NHL amended the icing rule to its current form, a so-called "hybrid" rule. Pursuant to this rule, no player will touch the puck to determine whether icing should be called. Although this rule does not create the same level of anticipation as the prior icing rule, and we have seen more than one bad call on this rule given that it requires a lot of discretion on the part of the officials. But, after seeing some of the horrible injury-inducing hits under the prior icing rules, the trade-off is undoubtedly worth it.

Under the hybrid icing rule, the officials signal that there is potential for icing (hand/arm straight up in the air) when the puck is shot down the ice across the goal line on either side of the net as described above. Then, the players skate in a race to be the first to approach the puck. However, when the players get close to the faceoff circle nearest the puck, the officials will determine which player reached the faceoff circle first. The players are not given the opportunity to actually skate up to and touch the puck for purposes of icing. If the officials determine that a player from the potentially offending team reached the circle first, the play will continue with no whistle. If the officials determine that someone from the other team reached the circle first, they will call icing by blowing the whistle to stop play. Though this rule would seem to have little discretion, some interpretation does arise as to who arrives at the appropriate faceoff circle first.

When icing is called, the offending team does not receive a penalty, but they do have three significant consequences. First, the faceoff to restart play will occur in that team's defensive zone. Although, the team can decide at which defensive zone faceoff dot the post-icing faceoff will occur. Second, the offending team is not allowed to change any of the players on the ice with any players on the bench until after the post-icing faceoff. This means that the five players who were on the ice when the puck was iced must stay on the ice until after play resumes. Third, the offending team may not take a timeout after icing.

The main goal of an icing call is to prevent a team from slowing or halting gameplay (i.e. preventing the other team from making an offensive play or continuing offensive pressure) by shooting the puck down the ice to the other end of the arena. The league has tweaked the icing rules to further support this goal throughout the years. The defensive zone faceoff, no-line-change, and no timeout consequences (i.e. no rest) tend to deter teams from intentionally icing the puck in most circumstances. This is intended to further discourage teams from using icing as a way to disrupt offensive pressure, in other words, to limit use of icing as a defensive tool. That notwithstanding, there are circumstances in which a player may deem the offensive threat to be so significant that he will incur the consequences by intentionally icing the puck.

What is offsides?

Offside (commonly referred to as "offsides") occurs when: (1) a player crosses his team's offensive blue line before the puck does, and (2) the player or one of his teammates touches the puck in the offensive zone. The rule is that the puck must cross the blue line *before* any attacking player. If a player was in the offensive zone before the puck or appears to be crossing the line before the puck, the linesmen will signal such by putting their arm/hand straight up in the air at the blue line.

Offsides may be committed by the player with control of the puck or one of his teammates who enters the offensive zone before the player controlling the puck. If a player is already in the offensive zone and the puck enters it, the player must skate outside of the zone and then return to the zone or "touch up" before he or any of his teammates may touch the puck in the zone. If they touch the puck without leaving the zone, the officials will call offsides by blowing the whistle to stop play.

The main goal of an offsides call is to prevent what is called cherry-picking. This occurs when a player hovers in or near the offensive zone waiting for the puck to reach that area, rather than actively participating in the game at all ends of the arena and only skating toward the zone when the play is moving that way. Offsides calls tend to deter such activity because when an offsides call is made, the play is stopped. This halts the team's offensive momentum or play and moves the next faceoff outside the offensive zone. The faceoff typically will be in the neutral zone unless the offsides was determined to be intentional or there was a delayed penalty before offsides was called, in which case the faceoff will be in the offending team's defensive zone.

Who are the guys in stripes and who's on the headset?

Officiating in a hockey game occurs on and off the ice. Off-ice review comes from the "Situation Room" in Toronto (for video review and replays). If the officials are using a headset from the ice in front of the area between the penalty boxes, they typically are talking to the Situation Room. On the ice, there are typically four officials—two linesmen and two referees. The linesmen focus on the location of the puck, mostly when it enters and leaves a zone, monitoring things like offsides and icing. Only the linesmen call icing or offsides, unless something prevents a linesman from being able to perform his duties (such as if he is knocked over), in which case a ref may stand in for that linesman. A linesman will report certain actions to the refs, but also is responsible for reviewing and stopping play when certain infractions occur, such as when a goal occurs on an illegal play, when a puck is out of bounds (i.e. over the glass or into a bench), or when there is a hand pass.

The refs tend to follow the general play more closely, including near each net to determine whether a goal is good. Additionally, one of refs will drop the puck for the initial faceoff of each period and after each goal. In other circumstances, the linesmen typically handle the faceoffs. The refs also announce the result of any on-ice review, such as a coach's challenge or waiving off a goal, and the result of any review by the Situation Room. Because the officials see things from different angles, sometimes the linesmen will report penalties to the refs or the refs will consult one another to confirm whether a penalty should be called, against whom, and what penalty should be assessed.

Certain plays can be reviewed by the Situation Room. Off-ice review typically occurs when determining whether a certain play resulted in a good goal. The team in Toronto can review various video playbacks from myriad angles to help determine whether the puck crossed the line and/or whether a goal was invalid due to an illegal play or penalty (such as high stick or goalie interference). If a goal is made on an illegal play, it is not a good goal and it will not be counted.

Importantly, a call made on the ice—goal or no goal—is the presumption. For the Situation Room to suggest overturning a decision called on the ice, they must have "clear" evidence that the on-ice decision was inaccurate or missed something that the video replay shows. This means that if a call is borderline and cannot be definitively determined, the call on the ice will stand.

In recent years, the league has given coaches a "coach's challenge." Each coach is allowed one per game. The exact scope and approach of these challenges have been altered slightly over the past few years. The coach's challenge allows a coach to challenge a play that otherwise would not have been reviewed by the control room. For example, a coach may challenge a goal if the coach believes the puck was brought into the zone offside in the play immediately preceding the goal, but the on-ice officials failed to call offsides. If a coach were to make such challenge, the Situation Room would review the video playback from the time the puck was brought into the zone before the purported goal. If it was determined that the puck was brought into the zone offside, any resulting goal would be overturned or invalidated, and the coach's challenge would have been successful. If it is determined that the puck was not brought in offside, the challenge would be rejected, the coach would lose his ability to challenge any other play in the game, and the team would receive a minor penalty. Because of the risk of incurring a penalty, coach's challenges typically are used sparingly or when the coach and his coaching team have a reasonable degree of confidence that they saw an illegal play. Sometimes players will give recommendations to coaches as well. For example, a goalie may tell his coach if he felt that he was interfered with when a goal went in the net.

Each game also has some off-ice officials. This includes: an official scorer, who tracks the players and their goals and assists; an official timekeeper, who monitors the time and makes adjustments when necessary, such as in the case of "false starts" on the faceoff; a penalty timekeeper, who tracks penalties and monitors the start/expiration of them; real-time scorers, who track the statistics for goalies and skaters (shots on goal, goals, assists, etc.); and a video goal judge, who is the designated official in Toronto to handle video reviews, including reviewing all goals.

What are penalties and how do you know one has occurred?

The officials constantly monitor the game for penalties. If a player commits a penalty—an illegal infraction—during gameplay that a ref can see, the ref will put his arm straight up into the air. If the offending player's team has control of the puck, the ref will blow the whistle to stop play. If the other team has control of the puck, play will continue until the offending player's team touches the puck. This is called a delayed penalty.

There are several different classifications of penalties. These include minor penalties, double minor penalties, bench minor penalties, coincidental penalties, major penalties, misconduct or game misconduct penalties, and match penalties. There also may be a penalty shot. The specific penalties are outlined below.

When a player receives a penalty, he is required to sit in the penalty box for a period of time to serve the penalty. The penalty times are two minutes for a minor, four minutes for a double minor, and five minutes for a major. A misconduct penalty is ten minutes, but the player will typically serve such a penalty off-ice in the locker room. A match penalty is for the remainder of the game.

If a penalty is a bench penalty, the penalty is assessed against the team rather than a specific player. In such cases, the team can select which player will serve the penalty for the team. If the goalie commits a penalty, another player will serve on the goalie's behalf.

What is a delayed penalty?

If a team has control of the puck and one of the team's players is the victim of a penalty, the ref will seek to call a penalty. This will be signified by extending his arm straight up above his head. However, as long as the non-offending team has control of the puck, the play will continue. This is called a delayed penalty. During this time, the non-offending team can bring onto the ice an extra skater ("extra attacker") if they call their goalie to the bench ("pull the goalie"). This would make the play six-on-five (if both teams were full-strength before the delayed penalty occurred). This gives the non-offending team extra time with an additional player. If the non-offending team scores while the delayed penalty is in effect, the penalty will be extinguished. On the other hand, if the offending team is able to touch the puck with reasonable control (not just if the puck bounces off a skater on the offending team), the whistle will be blown, the delayed penalty will end, and the penalty will begin.

What happens if someone gets a penalty?

When a penalty is assessed, the team with the offending player plays with one skater down, or "short-handed." Typically, the disadvantaged team will play with 4 skaters for the duration of the penalty. That team is said to be on the penalty kill, while the benefitting team is on the power play. Each team has specific lines of players who serve on penalty kills and power plays. These are called special teams.

Although a team's approach and game style look different during a penalty, the game rules are largely the same as during regular play. Yet, there is one significant difference: the shorthanded team is permitted to ice the puck as many times as it wishes during a penalty kill without any stoppage in play. Teams often ice the puck or send one player to skate the puck down into the offensive zone, when possible during the penalty kill. The team would welcome a short-handed goal, but the real intent is to control the puck and "run the clock" on the penalty time.

If the teams are not both full-strength (five skaters each) when a penalty is called, the composition of the teams may be different than the usual four-on-five skater composition. For example, if a team is playing with only four skaters when a penalty is called while the other team has five skaters, the team will go down to three skaters and will play three-on-five. When the first penalty expires (the time runs out), that team will play four-on-five. By way of another example, if the teams are playing four-on-four when a penalty is called on one team, the penalized team will play three-on-four until the initial penalties expire. Following the first whistle after the initial penalties expire, the teams will switch to four-on-five play for the remainder of the penalty.

As to goals during a penalty, if the short-handed team scores on their penalty kill, they get a shorthanded goal or "shortie." If the team on the power play scores, they get a power play goal. The effect of either is the same as a regular goal, but they have different designations in the scorekeeping. When a power play goal is scored, a minor penalty will end—regardless how much time was remaining. On the other hand, even if a power play goal is scored during a major or double minor, that penalty will continue until the full penalty time is completed.

Although the above describes the typical structure, there are three main exceptions to this structure: (1) a player on the other team gets a penalty as well (coincidental or not), (2) the penalty is a misconduct for ten+ minutes or a match penalty, or (3) a penalty shot is awarded.

Can each team get a penalty at the same time?

Yes. Coincidental penalties exist when one player from each team is penalized at the same time. In that situation, both players receive a penalty and the teams play four-on-four until the penalties expire. Even if one team scores, neither of the penalties will expire. If both teams have a penalty, but the penalties were not called concurrently, a penalty will end if a goal is scored.

However, penalties do not need to be assessed concurrently against both teams. If one team is on the penalty kill and the power play team engages in a penalty, the officials will assess the penalty for the full time starting when it is called. For example, if team A is on the penalty kill with 1:45 remaining on the penalty when one of team B's players commits an infraction, the officials will call the penalty in the ordinary course (meaning as soon as team B touches the puck, they will blow the whistle). If the whistle is blown when team A has 1:30 left on the penalty kill, team B's penalty will start at that time and continue for 30 seconds after team A's penalty expires, giving team A a thirty-second power play once their penalty expires. When both teams are shorthanded (whether coincidental or not), all other game rules apply. Most notably, when the teams are equally shorthanded, such as if they are playing four-on-four, the standard icing rules apply—the teams are simply playing the normal game with one fewer players.

What is a misconduct penalty?

Misconduct and match penalties are different from minor or major penalties. A standard misconduct penalty is ten minutes and is assessed when a player commits a penalty egregiously or commits multiple penalties (sometimes during the course of a short span of time). When a misconduct penalty is assessed, the offending player will sit in the penalty box or may go back to the locker room, but his team is not shorthanded. If a goalie commits a misconduct penalty, any player who was on the ice at the time of the penalty can serve the penalty for the goalie. A match penalty or game misconduct penalty is typically assessed when there is intent to injure, egregious behavior, or repeated bad behavior. When assessed, the player is removed from the rest of the game.

What is a penalty shot?

Officials may award a penalty shot rather than a standard penalty under certain circumstances. Penalty shots are quite rare in NHL games. A penalty shot can be awarded to a team instead of a powerplay when a player is prevented from a scoring chance by an opposing player committing a penalty. One of the most common examples occurs when a player is stopped from shooting while on a breakaway because another player commits a penalty against him.

To illustrate the breakaway penalty shot example: player X intercepts a pass between defensemen of the opposing team and skates in front of them on the breakaway with the puck toward the goalie at the other end. Then, when player X gets into position to shoot on the goalie one-on-one, one of the opposing team's defensemen comes up behind player X and trips him. If the officials determine that player X had a scoring opportunity that was prevented by the trip, they will award player X a penalty shot.

When a penalty shot is called, player X is given the opportunity to shoot at the goalie one-on-one.

The other players leave the ice and wait on the bench. Then, player X will skate toward the goalie with the puck starting from the red line, and player X will have the chance to shoot on the goalie. Player X must be the one to take the penalty shot, he cannot have another player substitute for him. If player X scores a goal on the penalty shot, it will be added to the team score and the play will resume from the faceoff circle at center ice as it would after any other goal. If a goal is not scored, the play will resume from a faceoff circle in that end or zone.

Notably, when taking a penalty shot, the player is subject to the same rules as would apply during a shootout, except that a spin-o-rama move (when a player spins around while skating toward the goal) is not permitted. The goalie must stay in his crease until the player touches the puck. As soon as the player touches the puck, the goalie is free to move around, cutoff the player's angle, or prevent the shot. Of course, the goalie may not dislodge the net or throw his stick or any of his equipment toward the puck. The goalie's team may not try to distract the shooter; if they do, the player will get another penalty shot, the team will be assessed a minor penalty, and the interfering player may get a misconduct penalty.

What acts are considered penalties?

Minor penalties include: charging, cross-checking, delay of game, high-sticking, holding (or holding the stick), hooking, interference, roughing, slashing, tripping, elbowing, unsportsmanlike conduct, and too many men on the ice. A minor penalty can become a double minor penalty if the action causes the other player to bleed. The most common example occurs when one player high-sticks another player in the face and the affected player bleeds as a result of getting hit by the stick. The offending player will then get a double minor. Intent does not matter. Though officials have some discretion, such as if a player exaggerates a fall (see diving/embellishment below). Given that intent is not required for a minor penalty, players are expected to play in a manner so as to minimize potential penalties (such as by keeping their sticks on the ice to avoid incidental contact with the stick, triggering a high-sticking call).

Major penalties include: boarding, illegal check to the head, checking from behind, fighting, spearing, or any minor penalty with intent to cause injury. Except in the case of fighting, all major penalties are reviewed in real time by the referee using video replays. Toronto does not review or provide guidance on these calls.

Game misconduct could include severe or repeated conduct of other types of penalties, such as clipping, charging, or getting three major penalties in a game.

Players may also get penalties of varying degrees if they use illegal equipment. The most common of these penalties is when a player continues to play with a broken stick. A player is expected to immediately drop a stick when it breaks. If the player does not immediately drop the stick, he will receive a minor penalty.

Certain penalties (or a succession of penalties over a period of time) can result in automatic fines or penalties. Other penalties are subject to review within the discretion of the NHL Commissioner's office for potential fines or game suspensions.

There are many different actions or behaviors that constitute penalties. Some of the more common ones are noted below with a brief explanation.

Boarding

Pushing, checking, or tripping a player into the boards aggressively.

Charging

Taking multiple strides toward a player before checking him violently.

Checking from Behind

Checking a player who has his back toward you.

Clipping

Making contact with a player at or below the knees either by lowering your body or leaving your feet.

Cross-checking

Holding your stick with both hands and using your stick to check another player.

Delay of Game

This penalty can take a few forms. Some common examples are when a player intentionally knocks his goal off of its posts or when a player flips the puck over the glass while the play is in his defensive zone.

Diving

> Also known as <u>embellishment</u>. This is when a player tries to "sell" to the officials that he is the victim of a penalty. A player can get this penalty for pretending to be injured/fall or over-exaggerating a fall/injury.

Elbowing

> Using an elbow to make contact with a player.

High-sticking

> Hitting a player with a raised stick (above the shoulders), regardless whether intentional or inadvertent. (As noted above, this also describes an illegal goal whereby someone bats the puck into the net with his stick at a height above the crossbar.)

Holding

> Holding or grabbing a player, whether the body, jersey, stick, or otherwise.

Hooking

> Use of a stick blade to grab or "hook" a player, usually to slow the player down.

Interference

Checking or making other contact with a player who does not have the puck (and did not just pass it). If a player checks someone who had just passed the puck within the preceding few seconds and the player had momentum which would make avoiding the check difficult, this usually is not called as interference.

Kneeing

Using the knee to make contact with another player.

Roughing

Excessive pushing or aggressive contact, especially after the whistle

Too Many Men

A team has more than five skaters (or more than the number of skaters permitted based on any penalties) on the ice. There is a bit of leeway to allow for changing on the fly. However, if one of the new players touches the puck or gets into the play before the player he is replacing leaves the ice, the penalty will be called.

Tripping

Using a stick or leg to trip a player. Using a leg to trip a player may also be called a "slew foot," which is considered more severe than normal tripping.

Unsportsmanlike Conduct

This penalty can take a few forms. Examples include using profanity or obscene gestures, grabbing a player's mask, or throwing objects onto the ice.

How can I tell what the officials are signaling?

It can take some time before it becomes natural to watch the gameplay and the officials simultaneously. Once a penalty is called, an official will move to center ice and identify the penalty by using hand gestures. It is true that the penalty also is usually announced over the PA system and by TV announcers. However, it's still helpful to understand what the hand gestures mean. Below is a brief explanation of the gestures associated with penalties, plus some images for illustration.

<u>Boarding</u>: One hand is a fist that punches the other open hand.

<u>Checking from Behind</u>: Push arms straight out away from body to full extension.

<u>Charging</u>: Hold arms perpendicular to body, make fists, and rotate fists around forearms away from the body.

<u>Cross-checking</u>: Two fists pushed straight out in front of the body.

Delay of Game: Lift arm straight out to the side.

High-sticking: Put both hands near the face as if holding a stick up in the air at an angle.

Elbowing: Lift one arm up with the elbow at a right angle and that hand toward the ceiling. Then put the other hand beneath the elbow.

Holding: Lift one arm in front of and across the body and put the other hand on the forearm.

Hooking: As if holding a stick near the waist, pull the "stick" toward the body.

Match: One open hand on head.

Interference: Arms crossed in front of body in an X.

Misconduct: Hands on hips.

<u>Kneeing</u>: Tap the knee with either hand.

<u>Roughing</u>: Push one arm out to the side of the body.

<u>Slashing</u>: Hold one arm out in front of and across the body and making a karate chop motion with the other hand onto the forearm.

<u>Unsportsmanlike Conduct</u>: Make a "T" with the hands in front of the body. (Same as "Timeout.")

Spearing: As if holding a stick at the waist, push the "stick" away from the body.

Tripping: Bend slightly and move arm down in a sweeping motion from front to back.

Following are some of the other hand signals that officials may use to designate infractions (or potential infractions) which do not constitute penalties:

Delayed Penalty:
Non-whistle arm
extended above
the head.

Icing: One official extends his arm straight into the air (see "Delayed Penalty" image). If icing is assessed, second official will extend arm straight into the air, blow the whistle, then skate to the new faceoff dot, and cross his arms.

Goal: Point to the net with arm extended.

Timeout: Same as "Unsportsmanlike Conduct."

Hand Pass: Open hand pointing down to ice with left to right movement.

Washout/Waive-off: Lifting each arm straight out to either side after crossing in the middle with palms facing down.

When is a goal not a goal?

In most cases, when the puck goes into the opposing team's net a goal is scored. But that is not always the case. There are some nuances to that. Most importantly, the puck must completely cross the goal line at the front of the net to count as a goal. The puck does not have to cross the line while physically on the ice and it does not have to stay in the net once it has crossed the line. Even if the puck bounces out of the net, it still counts. However, if the puck stops on the goal line or does not fully cross it, there is no goal.

There are certain circumstances that can cause an official to waive off a goal. For example, if the puck is batted into the net with a high stick or otherwise goes into the net off a high stick, generally there is no goal. Specifically, if the puck was directed into the net by the stick (usually the blade or lower shaft of the stick) while the stick was above the crossbar, any purported goal will not count.

By way of another example, if the puck is kicked into the net, there is no goal. A player is permitted to direct the puck into net with his skate as long as there is no "distinct kicking motion." If there is any kicking motion, the goal will be invalidated.

As yet another example, if the goalie was interfered with when the puck entered the net, there will be no goal. Whether a goalie was sufficiently interfered with in order to waive off a goal will depend on whether the goalie was deprived an opportunity to move or potentially make a save in his crease because of a skater's interference. The key point is that players have an obligation to avoid contact with a goalie to the extent possible. If the goalie is interfered with such that he is unable to move to make a save, any resulting goal will not count. However, if one of the goalie's teammates is at fault for any such interference, as long as the interfering player tried to avoid interfering with the goalie or had no way to avoid contact with the goalie, there will be no interference call and the goal will count.

To illustrate the example in the preceding paragraph, offensive player Z is skating toward the goalie to shoot, while defending player A trips player Z, causing player Z to crash into the goalie and sending the puck into the net. If player Z attempted to redirect himself so he did not run into the goalie or otherwise had no opportunity to avoid the collision, he will not be faulted for player A's defensive action, and any resulting goal likely will be awarded. But, if player Z did nothing to avoid or mitigate his contact with the goalie when it was deemed that he could have done so, the resulting goal likely will not be awarded.

How are players evaluated?

Players are evaluated based on many different elements. However, the most common elements are goals scored, assists made, and plus/minus rating. Each is discussed in turn.

When a goal is scored, the last attacking skater to touch the puck is credited with the goal. This is true regardless of the way the skater touched the puck—shot it into the net, touched the puck on a redirection, or even if the puck bounces off of the skater. If the puck bounces off the defending team and into the net, the last offensive skater to have shot or touched the puck is the scorer.

Up to two players may get an "assist" on a goal. If a skater scores when shooting the puck and the last person before him to touch the puck was someone on the other team, the skater's goal is deemed to have been "unassisted." This is common on a breakaway goal. An assist occurs when the player has control of or touches the puck immediately before the goal scorer and passes (or directs) the puck to the goal-scorer. A second assist occurs if a player has control of or touches the puck immediately before the person who gets the first assist and passes the puck to the player who then passes it to the goal-scorer. If a player on the other team touches the puck between the player passing and a skater then scores a goal on that play, the passing players will not get an assist on that goal.

Players also receive a plus/minus or +/- rating. The plus/minus rating is calculated based on goals scored while a player is on the ice. If a goal is scored for the player's team while the player is on the ice, the player earns 1 (+1). If a goal is scored against the player's team while the player is on the ice, the player loses 1 (-1). The plus/minus rating is the overall total that the player has from among all games of that season.

How are teams ranked?

As noted above, games never end in a tie. If a game is tied at the end of the three regular periods, an overtime period will be played. If the game remains tied after the overtime period, the game will go to a shootout. These will be discussed in the next section. If a team wins a game, regardless whether in regular time, overtime, or the shootout, the team receives two points. If a team loses a game in regular time, that losing team receives zero points. However, if a game goes into overtime or a shootout, the losing team receives one point. The points are used to determine each team's standing (ranking) in its division and the league. The standings ultimately determine which teams participate in playoffs for the Stanley Cup at the end of the season, as well as who plays who.

How does the game end?

If a game is tied at the end of regular time (three periods) during the regular season, the game will move to an overtime period. The overtime period will be up to five minutes long. During overtime, the teams will play three-on-three instead of five-on-five. This is a sudden death overtime. The first team to score wins the game, regardless how much time is left in the overtime period.

If a game is still tied at the end of the overtime period, the players will participate in a shootout. In a shootout, each team will pick three skaters to shoot against the other team's goalie one-on-one. The home team will decide whether they or the away team shoots first. As noted above, this is like the penalty shot—when it is his turn, each skater will start at the red line in the center and skate toward the goalie with the hope of scoring. The skater must continue to skate forward towards the goalie. Skaters participating in the shootout may not skate backwards at any time and may not stop. After the first skater completes his attempt, whether he scored or not, the other team's first skater will then attempt to score on the other team's goalie. The team with the most goals from the first three attempts wins. If the score is tied between the two teams at the end of the first round with three skaters/attempts each, the teams will then take turns allowing one more of its skaters to attempt to score. The first team to break the tie, if the other team doesn't score also, will win.

To illustrate shootout scoring: if the score is tied 2-2 at the end of the initial frame of three skaters/attempts each, one frame of one skater per team will be added. If the first team to shoot scores during the fourth frame, the second team also must score to force a fifth frame, or they will lose. On the other hand, if the first team to shoot does not score during the fourth frame, but the second team does, the game will end with the second team being declared the winner. If neither team scores, an additional frame will be added. This will continue until a winner is determined.

For many years, if the game was tied after the five-minute overtime period, the game ended in a tie. In the 2005-06 season, the league implemented the overtime and shootout process as described above. The process remains controversial for many hockey fans who believe that a shootout does not accurately portray which team played better and which team truly "won" the game. However, the league determined that (a) ties were inappropriate and (b) multiple overtime periods were too physically demanding for players over the course of eighty-two games. Accordingly, the shootout format was created. Yet, given the controversy, this method of determining winners only occurs during regular season.

During playoffs, there is no shootout. Rather, the teams will play full additional periods of the game until a team scores. Additionally, the teams play five-on-five for each overtime period. If the game is tied at the end of three regular periods, there will be an additional period of twenty minutes (after cleaning the ice, as would normally occur between the first/second and the second/third periods). If no team scores during the first overtime period, it will be followed by another full overtime period and so on, until a team scores. In other words, playoffs games can and will continue through multiple overtime periods until a winner is declared.

Which teams compete in the playoffs?

Sixteen of the NHL's thirty-one teams (thirty-two once Seattle's team is incorporated) will participate in the playoffs. The teams that participate in the playoffs are selected based on team point totals. The top three teams in each division participate in the playoffs. Additionally, there are two "wild card" spots for each conference. This results in a total of eight teams from each conference (three from each of the conference's two divisions, plus two wild card teams). Wild card spots are given to the two teams with the next-highest point totals from among all teams in that conference (regardless of division).

In the event that there is a tie among potential playoff-eligible teams, the tie will be broken based on the team that has won the most games in regular time or overtime (in other words, it excludes shootout wins). For example, if two teams competing for the third slot (i.e. to be the third best) in the division, and both have the same number of points, the league will review how each team earned those points. Records can be read as follows: Wins-Losses-Overtime Losses.

By way of example, let's consider an example where two teams have 100 points each. One team has the following record: 46-28-8. This team's points are calculated as: (46 wins x 2 points = 92 points) + (8 overtime losses x 1 point = 8 points) = 100 total points. The first team won 3 of its 46 winning games in the shootout, so it has a total of 43 non-shootout wins. The second team has the following record: 44-26-12. This team's points are calculated as: (44 wins x 2 points = 88 points) + (12 overtime losses x 1 point = 12 points) = 100 total points. The second team did not win any games in the shootout, so it has a total of 44 of non-shootout wins. Although the first team has more overall wins, it has fewer non-shootout wins (43 vs. 44), so the second team will take the third slot for its division.

If the teams remained tied after considering non-shootout wins, such as if both of the teams had won exactly 43 games outside of a shootout, they are next evaluated based on their head-to-head record (i.e which team won more games against the other). If they played four games, and the first team won three of the four games, they get the third slot. If the teams remain tied after this (meaning that both won the same number of games against the other), the final tiebreaker is goal differential. The goal differential is the calculation of the number of goals a team has scored minus the number of goals that have been scored against that team. For example, if a team has scored 200 goals, but it has had 190 goals scored against it, it's goal differential would be 10. By way of another example, if a team has scored 200 goals, but it has 210 goals scored against it, its goal differential is -10. For tie breaking, the team with the highest goal differential would take the third slot.

How do playoffs work?

Once the playoff slots have been determined, the teams are matched up within their own conference based on standing. In each conference, the team with the most points will play the second wild card team (which typically has the fewest points of the teams from that conference), the other team that won its division (i.e. had the best record in its division) will play the first wild card team, and the team that was second in its division will play the team that was third in that same division. In round 2, the team that wins the match-up between the number one and the second wild card team will play the team that wins the match-up between the winner of the second-place and third-place teams in that division, while the team that wins the match-up between the other division's first-place team and the first wild card team will play the team that wins the match-up between the winner of the second- and third-place teams in that division. Then, in round 3, the winners from each division match-up will play one another. Then that winner will play in the Stanley Cup finals against the winner of the other conference. In the finals, the team with the better regular season record, regardless of division standing, will have the home ice advantage. The number one team in the league will have home ice advantage in all four rounds, assuming the team plays in all four rounds.

In each round, the teams will play the best out of seven. In a match-up, the team that wins four games advances to the next round and the other team is eliminated. The team with the higher standing in each match-up will have the home ice advantage. This means that the first two games are played at home, the next two are away, the fifth is home, the sixth is away, and the seventh is home. Of course, this assumes that each team has won three games to force a game seven. There could be any configuration of games. A team could win in a "sweep", meaning that they win all of the first 4 games played. There is an advantage to winning in fewer games—that team has a longer break until the next round because the next round will not start until after the other matchups in that conference are completed. A playoff bracket illustrating these rounds is on the following page.

The teams that advance past the first round go to the second round or quarter-finals. The teams that win in the second round go to the third round, or the semi-finals. The teams that participate in the semi-finals also are deemed the winners of their respective conferences. The teams that win in the semi-finals will go to the finals, where one team from each conference plays against the other.

The team that wins in the finals, the last round of the playoffs, wins the Stanley Cup ("the Cup"). The names of each qualifying player and qualifying staff member from each winning team are etched onto the outside of the Cup. The Cup includes all known players from 1893-1923. The league began engraving all of the winning team members each year starting in 1924.

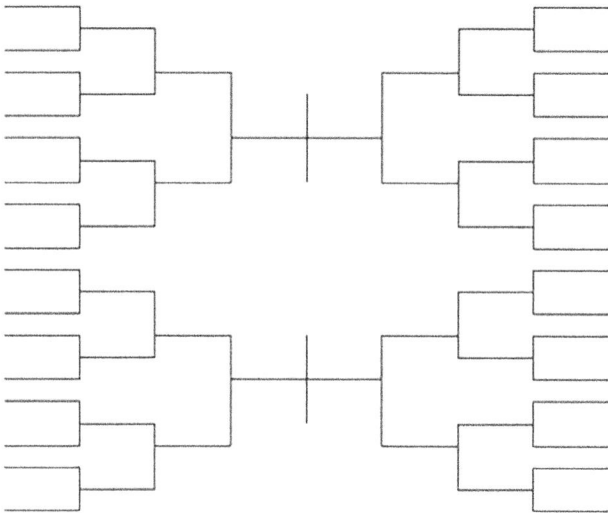

What are all the awards?

Though the Stanley Cup is the most well-known, there are many awards and trophies. Below is a list of the awards, including the date each was first awarded and an interesting fact about each.

Stanley Cup

As stated above, it is awarded to the team that wins the final round of the playoffs in a season. The Cup has had a few names, starting with the Dominion Hockey Challenge Cup. Ultimately, it was named after Lord Stanley of Preston, who was Governor General of Canada. Lord Stanley donated the Cup in 1892. It had been awarded to Canada's best amateur hockey club until 1909, when competition for the Cup was limited to professional teams. In 1926, the competition was further limited only to NHL teams.

When a team wins the Cup, the Cup is shown at various team/league promotional events. There is a widely followed superstition among players that if you touch the Cup during a year that you did not win the Cup, you will be jinxed and will not win the Cup. Accordingly, you won't see a player touch the Cup unless/until he hoists it as part of a Cup-winning team. In a unique tradition, when a team wins the Cup, each player takes possession of the Cup for a day. The player can do whatever he wants with it. Many players bring it to their hometowns and share it with local fans, some eat/drink out of it, others put their kids or pets in it—creativity is the only real limit.

President's Trophy

Awarded to the team with the best record overall (i.e. most points) at the end of the regular season. The winning team is guaranteed home-ice advantage in all four rounds of the playoffs. However, superstition says that the team who wins the President's Trophy is cursed and will not win the Cup. The President's Trophy has been awarded each year since 1985-86, but only eight of the Trophy winners have gone on to win the Cup in the same year that they won the Trophy.

Divisional Titles

The team with the most points in its division at the end of the regular season is the champion for that division.

Prince of Wales Trophy

Awarded to the team that is the playoff champion in the Eastern Conference, in other words, the team that wins the semi-finals for the Eastern Conference. It was first awarded in the 1925-26 season.

Clarence D. Campbell Bowl

Awarded to the team that is the playoff champion in the Western conference, in other words, the team that wins the semi-finals for the Western Conference. The trophy was physically created in 1878, but was not first awarded until the 1967-68 season.

Conn Smythe

Awarded to the most valuable player for his team during the playoffs. Members of the Professional Hockey Writers' Association vote to elect the player following the last game of the playoffs, and the trophy is awarded to the winner just before the Cup is awarded. It was first awarded in the 1964-65 season. Patrick Roy has won it three times.

Hart Memorial Trophy:

Awarded to the most valuable player for his team throughout the season. The Professional Hockey Writers' Association members select their top five picks for the trophy, and then announce three finalists. The winner is announced at a formal awards ceremony, the NHL Awards, which has been held in Las Vegas in recent years (even before Vegas had a team). It has been awarded since the 1923-24 season. Wayne Gretzky holds the record for multiple wins, having won the trophy nine times. The trophy has only been awarded to a goalie eight times, with Dominic Hasek winning it twice.

Calder Memorial Trophy

Awarded to the best rookie in the regular season. The Professional Hockey Writers' Association members select their top five picks for the trophy, and then announce three finalists. The winner is announced at the NHL Awards. It has been awarded since the 1936-37 season.

Vezina Trophy

Awarded to the best goalie in the regular season. The Professional Hockey Writers' Association members select their top five picks for the trophy, and then announce three finalists. The winner is announced at the NHL Awards. It has been awarded since the 1926-27 season. From 1946-47 to 1981-82, it was awarded not to the overall "best" goalie, but to the goalie who had allowed the fewest goals during the season. There is now a separate trophy for the goalie with the fewest goals (the William M. Jennings Trophy). Under the current method of evaluating candidates for the trophy, Dominik Hasek has won Vezina Trophy the most times at six.

James Norris Memorial Trophy

Awarded to the best all-around defenseman. The Professional Hockey Writers' Association members select their top five picks for the trophy, and then announce three finalists. The winner is announced at the NHL Awards. It has been awarded since the 1953-54 season. Only two players have won both the Hart and the Norris Trophy in the same season—Bobby Orr (1969-70, 1970-71, and 1971-72 seasons) and Chris Pronger (1999-2000 season).

Art Ross Trophy

Awarded to the player with the most points in the regular season. Wayne Gretzky has won 10 times, Gordie Howe and Mario Lemieux have each won six times, and Phil Esposito and Jaromir Jagr have each won five times. Only one American player has won the award—Patrick Kane in 2016. In quite a feat, Stan Mikita won the Art Ross, Hart, and the Lady Byng trophies twice (the 1966-67 season and the 1967-68 season). No other player has won all three in one season.

Frank J. Selke Trophy

Awarded to the best defensive forward. The Professional Hockey Writers' Association members select their top five picks for the trophy, and then announce three finalists. The winner is announced at the NHL Awards. It has been awarded since the 1977-78 season. It has been won four times by both Bob Gainey (the first four seasons the trophy was awarded) and by Patrice Bergeron (2012, 2014, 2015, and 2017).

Lady Byng Memorial Trophy

Awarded to the most sportsmanlike and gentlemanly player with a high playing ability.

The Professional Hockey Writers' Association members select their top five picks for the trophy, and then announce three finalists. The winner is announced at the NHL Awards. It has been awarded since the 1924-25 season. The trophy was donated to the NHL by Lady Byng, Marie Evelyn Moreton, who was married to Viscount Byng of Vimy, the Governor General of Canada from 1921 to 1926. Lady Byng gave Frank Boucher the original trophy to keep after he won it seven times in eight years. She then donated a second trophy to the NHL in 1935-36.

Jack Adams

Awarded to the best coach, meaning the one who contributed most to his team's success during the regular season. The members of the National Hockey League Broadcasters select their top five picks for the trophy, and then announce three finalists. The winner is announced at the NHL Awards. It has been awarded since the 1972-73 season. Pat Burns has won the most, with three wins.

Maurice "Rocket" Richard Trophy

Awarded to the player with the most goals during the regular season. It has been awarded since the 1998-99 season. Unlike other awards, there is no tiebreaker, so multiple players can win it in one season. Alexander Ovechkin has won nine times.

King Clancy Memorial Trophy

Awarded to the player who shows on- and off-ice leadership and has made a humanitarian contribution in the community. A panel of members of the Professional Hockey Writers' Association and the NHL Broadcasters Association select their top five picks for the trophy, and then announce three finalists. The winner is announced at the NHL Awards. It has been awarded since the 1987-88 season. Only one player, Henrik Sedin, has won twice.

Ted Lindsay Award

Awarded to the most outstanding player as voted by players through the NHL Players' Association. Three finalists are announced and then the winner is announced at the NHL Awards. It has been awarded since the 1971-72 season, and it was called the Lester B. Peterson Award until 2010. Wayne Gretzky has won the award the greatest number of times with five wins.

William M. Jennings Trophy

Awarded to the goalie(s) who played at least twenty-five games with the team that has the fewest goals against during regular season. If the starting goalie and backup goalie for a team have each played at least twenty-five games, both goalies are declared winners of the trophy. It has been awarded since the 1981-82 season. Patrick Roy and Martin Brodeur have each won the award five times.

Mark Messier Leadership Award

Awarded to the player with great on-and off-ice leadership. Fans, teams, and NHL staff give suggestions to Mark Messier, who makes the decisions for the finalists and winner. The winner is announced at the NHL Awards. It has been awarded since the 2006-07 season.

Jim Gregory General Manager of the Year

Awarded to the GM of the year based on votes from a forty-one-person panel consisting of each team's GM, five NHL executives, and five media members. Three finalists are announced, and then the winner is announced at the NHL Awards. It has been awarded since 2010.

Bill Masterson Memorial Trophy

Awarded to the player who best shows perseverance, sportsmanship, and dedication to hockey. Each team nominates one player and then the Professional Hockey Writers' Association selects three finalists and the winner, with the winner being announced at the NHL Awards. It has been awarded since the 1967-68 season.

Where can I learn the lingo?

Following is a glossary with many of the terms you may hear from game announcers, other fans, and/or players. It includes some of the words we discussed in earlier parts of this book, plus some additional terms for reference.

B

Backchecking

When a player skates back to his defensive zone when the opposing team is on the rush, and the player guards one of the opposing players.

Backhander

A back-handed shot. One in which a player uses the back of the stick blade.

Bar Down

When a player shoots and the puck hits the bottom of the crossbar and it deflects down into the net.

Barn

The rink/arena.

Beauty or Beaut

A well-executed or good-looking shot.

Biscuit

Puck.

Block

When a player uses his body or equipment to stop a shot from reaching the net.

Blueliner

Defenseman.

Breadbasket

The goalie's chest. Typically, this is used when a player shoots and the puck hits the goalie's breadbasket (such as on the jersey logo).

Breakout

A team gets control of the puck in their defensive end and skates the puck into the offensive zone.

Breezers

Hockey pants.

Bucket

Helmet.

Butterfly

A style of goaltending where the goalie tends to play on his knees to cover the lower half of the net. Most goalies are now "hybrid" style which includes butterfly and standing.

C

Can-opener

When a player puts his stick between another player's legs and turns it.

Celly

(Pronounced like "selly".) A post-goal celebration.

Change

When one or more players goes off the ice and is replaced by one or more players from the bench.

Change on the fly

When one or more players is changed while play continues.

Check

A hit. May have different qualifiers (e.g., "hip check" = hit on the body using the hip).

Cherry picking

When a player lingers at center ice or just outside the offensive zone waiting for the puck rather than playing in his zone with his teammates.

Chiclets

Teeth (or lack thereof).

Chip

Often used in the phrases "chip in" or "chip off the boards." This means the puck is shot up off the ice into the zone or shot off the boards, respectively.

Chippy

When both teams start to take cheap shots on one another, the game has become chippy.

Chirp

Trash-talking toward an opponent or the officials. (As in "he's chirping the officials" or "those two are chirping each other.")

Clapper

A strong slapshot.

Clear the Puck

Shoot the puck out of the defensive zone to force the opposing team to leave your defensive zone.

Coast-to-coast

Play begins in the defensive zone near the net and is brought down the ice to the net in the offensive zone. Often results in a goal.

Crash the net

Players approaching the net with a lot of speed or power.

Crease

The blue painted semicircle in front of the net. Also called the goal crease.

Cycle

An offensive play to control the puck by passing it among players near the boards. A team will typically try to cycle the puck in the offensive zone until a teammate is near the net and open for a pass.

D

Dangle

When a player stick handles the puck in and around an opposing player or multiple opposing players.

Deke

A fake-out move. This is when a player tries to elude an opposing player. For example, a player may look at one of his teammates to make the opposing player believe he is going to pass the puck to that teammate, but the player instead handles a "no-look" pass to a different teammate.

Delayed Penalty

As described above, the officials may not stop play immediately when a penalty is identified if the team against which the infraction occurred has control of the puck. One of the officials will indicate whether there is a delayed penalty by holding his right arm straight up in the air.

Dots

The circles on the ice where the face-off occurs – the face-off dots.

Draw

The faceoff.

Drop the gloves

A player will physically take his gloves off and drop them on the ice to signify that he is willing to fight an opposing player. Also called "drop the mitts."

Dump-in

Shoot the puck into the offensive zone before crossing into the zone, not to anyone in particular. This is typically done to allow time for a line change or as part of a dump-and-chase.

Dump-and-Chase

A team will shoot the puck down into the offensive zone ("dump" the puck) and then its players will skate in after the puck ("chase" the puck).

E

Empty Net

When a team pulls its goalie (or when the goalie is out of his net).

Extra attacker

When a team pulls its goalie, they can add one more defenseman or forward to the ice. This person is an extra attacker.

F

Face wash

When a player puts his gloves into an opponent's face.

Fan

Used to describe when a player just misses making a pass or shot. As in, he "fanned on it."

Flow

Long hockey hair.

Five-hole

The scoring area on the goalie between his legs. It's called the five-hole because there are considered to be 5 main areas on the net/goalie where a player can score. The bottom left is 1, the bottom right is 2, the top right is 3, the top left is 4, and the area between the goalie's legs is 5.

Forecheck

Applying pressure on the opposing player/team to try to gain the puck while in your offensive zone.

Freeze the puck

When the goalie stops/traps the puck so it can't be played.

Full strength

When both teams have no players in the penalty box.

G

Game misconduct

> A penalty whereby a player is suspended for the rest of the game.

Garbage goal

> A goal scored after getting the puck on a rebound in or around the net.

Go-ahead goal

> A goal that puts the team ahead of the other team.

Goon

> A player who is an enforcer for a team. He responds when an opposing player engages in a dirty or aggressive play. He also may play when the teams get chippy. This player doesn't often get a lot of ice time.

Gordie Howe Hat Trick

> Gordie Howe was a legendary hockey player, in the ranks of Wayne Gretzky. A Gordie Howe Hat Trick is when a player has a goal, an assist, and gets into a fight in one game.

Grinder

> A player who plays physically, battles for the puck, and works hard. These players typically play on the third or fourth lines.

H

Hand pass

When a player passes the puck to another player using his hand. This is permitted in the defensive zone, but not in the neutral zone or offensive zone.

Hash marks

The lines near the edges of the face-off circles. Players can't enter the hash mark areas during face-offs.

Hat trick

When a player scores three goals in a game. Also called a "hatty." When a player scores three consecutive goals in one game, that is known as a "natural" or "pure" hat trick. (For a natural hat trick, it is irrelevant if the other team scores between the player's three consecutive goals.)

Headman

As in "headmanning the puck." Passing the puck to a teammate skating ahead of the player on the attack.

Hip check

Using one's hip to check an opponent.

Hoser

A person who is a loser.

House

The house is a specific area in front of the net –
from each post in a diagonal line to the faceoff
dot on either side, to the bottom of the faceoff
circle, and then straight across from the bottom
of each faceoff circle. This is where most goals
are scored.

I

Ice time

Time a player spends on-ice playing.

Interference

See section on penalties.

Lettuce

Good hockey hair. Also known as "salad." (See
also "flow".)

L

Light the lamp

Score a goal. (The red light behind the net lights
up when a goal is scored.)

Long change

The goalies change ends of the ice each period.
During periods one and three, the goalie is on
the end of the ice closest to his team's bench.
During the second period, the goalie is on the

end of the ice closest to the opposing team's bench. This means that during the second period, players have to skate to the other end of the ice to change players from their defensive zone.

M

Man advantage

When a team is on a power play, the team has a man advantage. If it's a five-on-three, they have a two-man advantage.

Mitts

A player's hands or a player's gloves.

N

Numbers

As in "they have numbers entering the zone." When a team has more offensive players moving into the zone than there are defensive players. See also Odd Man Rush.

O

Odd Man Rush

When the number of offensive players moving into the attacking zone is greater than the number of defensive players. Often referred to in terms of the numbers, such as a three-on-two (three offensive players against only two defensive players).

One-timer

Shooting the puck on net directly off of a pass from another player (or off the faceoff).

On-the-fly

A line change while the game is in play.

Open net

When the goalie is out of position or has left open all or part of the net.

P

Pinch

When a defenseman leaves the blue line and skates deeper into the offensive zone to play the puck, the defenseman is "pinching." It may also be called "pinching" when the defenseman tries to battle an opposing player at the blue line to try to keep the puck in the offensive zone.

Playmaker

A player known for stickhandling and passing - someone who makes a lot of plays to further the game.

Pipes

The goal posts.

Point
> The area just inside the blue line of the offensive zone. The defensemen usually hold these spots, but offensive players may rotate into those areas. Often used in the context of "pass to the point" or "he shot it from the point."

Pull the Goalie
> A team has its goalie leave the ice and sit on the bench. When it does so, the team can have another skater (an "extra attacker") on the ice.

R

Robbed
> When a player makes a great shot, but the goalie makes a great, unexpected save, the player was robbed.

S

Sauce
> Saucer pass. This is when the puck is passed to another player in the air (like a flying saucer).

Scoring chance
> When a player or the team has had a clear opportunity to score, such as if they are shooting from an area where goals frequently come from. This may include shots on goal or missed shots.

Screen

When one or more players in front of the net block the goalie from being able to see the puck coming at him, they were acting as a "screen."

Sieve

Pronounced like "give" with an "s" at the beginning instead of a "g". A bad goalie or a goalie playing poorly. This can be heard as a chant by fans taunting the other team's goalie.

Sin bin

The penalty box.

Short side

The side of the goal closest to the shooter. As in "that goal went in short side."

Shutout

When a goalie saves all shots against him so the other team has scored no goals in a game.

Slapshot

A hard shot with a long windup.

Snapshot

A quick shot from the wrist with little windup.

Snow

Buildup of the "shaved ice" from skates digging into the ice.

Slewfoot

When a player kicks out another player's legs. This is almost universally considered a dirty move.

Slot

> The area between the offensive zone faceoff circles and the crease (front of the goal). This is considered a great scoring area.

Snipe

> A strong or well-placed shot.

Sniper

> Someone known for making good shots/goals.

Special teams

> The players who are the lines on the power play or on the penalty kill are the "special teams."

Standing on one's head

> When a goalie is making big and/or good saves, the goalie is said to be standing on his head.

Stick check

> Defensive move using the stick to take possession or control of the puck from an attacking player. There are several variations. One common approach is to use your stick to lift another player's stick and then take the puck. Another common approach, called a poke check, occurs when a player uses the blade of his stick to "poke" the puck off of the other player's stick or otherwise out of his control.

Stickhandling

> Controlling the puck with the stick.

Sweater

> Hockey jersey.

T

Tag up

> Skate out to the neutral zone from the offensive zone when there is a delayed offside. Also called "touch up."

Tape-to-tape

> A pass from one player's stick blade to his teammate's stick blade with little effort.

Tender/Tendy

> The goalie.

Tic-tac-toe

> A series of tape-to-tape passes among teammates.

Top shelf

> The top two corners of the goal (areas 3 and 4). When a goal is scored by shooting the puck in such an area, the player is said to have "put it top shelf."

Traffic

> A lot of players in front of the net.

Turnover

> When one team intercepts a pass and takes control of the puck from the other team. The team that loses the puck has turned the puck over.

W

Waive off

When a stoppage of play is about to occur, such as in the case of icing, a referee may decide to continue play by "waving off" the icing. This can be done in different situations. For example, if the defenseman was pinching in in the offensive zone and he likely would've gotten the puck if it weren't for him pinching in, the ref may waive off the icing. This term also is used when a ref "waives off" a goal. This is when one might think a goal is scored, but the ref "waives it off" to signal that the puck actually did not cross the line.

Wrap-around

When a player takes the puck from near the net, around the back, and then to the other side of the net where he scores.

Printed in Great Britain
by Amazon